Requiem

BY

Alan Pemberton

*"Perhaps the greatest thing we can do for each other is to add
to joy and diminish pain"*

First published in 2002
By Requiem Press

120,Cavendish Place, Eastbourne, East Sussex, BN21 3 TZ
Email: mail@comfortpoetry.com
Website: www.comfortpoetry.com

Printed by Wessex Graphics of Gillingham Dorset

ISBN No 0-9543774-0-0

A CIP record of this book
Is available from the British Library

With grateful thanks to Paul McBride for the front cover image of the bench
and to Robert Weston for all his generous help in producing this book
Design by Andrew Niekirk

This book is dedicated to my children

Mark, John & Sara Lucy

' I am of no particular religious persuasion but I naturally and comfortably believe in a creative force, a Grand Architect, if you will, who fashioned this world and the infinite universe. I realised as a young boy that nothing is formed without thought. It logically followed that since this world is so beautifully composed, then so is the mind which created it!

I do not believe that we are designed, as humans, to understand the mysteries of life's origins. Brilliant minds have been driven insane in pursuit of answers. Acceptance allows harmony to grow unchallenged within us.

CONTENTS

Many Think It's Wrong

Many think it's wrong it seems
To speak at all of death
Birth is looked on joyously
Both are marked by breath
The first gasp of the infant
The last breath of the dying
Both of them are nothing more
Than Nature's loving sighing
To each a start
To each an end
So let there be no tears
The chains of life
Are freed by death
Along with doubts and fears
So we who have life
Can touch with love
The lives of those we meet
Leaving the souls who've travelled on
To sit at the Master's feet
For who are we to speculate
That death will not transcend
The fear we have of nothingness
That death must be the end
So do not think of darkness
When you grieve for those who've gone
They're just a little step ahead
The road we'll travel on

Heaven's Side

When the storm inside is raging
When the night has trapped your fears
When the nightmare starts unfolding
When you cannot stem your tears
I shall see you in your sorrow
I shall feel your deep despair
Softly fold my arms around you
Let you know that I am there
I have passed the veil of knowledge
Leaving you with earthly gloom
Heaven floats and flows between us
Death is neither end nor doom
In the sunshine of our memories
Spun by silver thread so fine
Lives a picture of our loving
All is saved which is divine
Hold our love which is forever
Call me and I'm by your side
Trust the voice you hear within you
Sending love from heaven's side

Veil Of Love

Sometimes they go badly wrong
The things we cherish most
Loved ones die or walk away
Bequeathing us their ghost
So loneliness or hateful hours
Can make us brood or pine
Resentments anger and despair
Can feed a sad decline
What can we do with sleepless nights
With fears we cannot still
How do we find that inner peace
When chaos rules our will
The golden thread which binds our soul
To mysteries beyond
Holds the key to happiness
And our immortal bond
No thing nor place nor person
Ensures our peace of mind
The One that understands us best
Is standing just behind
We do not need to travel
Or hide behind our tears

The veil of love is constant
More constant than our fears
For we can trust in every way
The Master's hand and power
The pulpit fashions evidence
The truth is in the flower
That we could put away our pride
The touchstone of our pain
And turn to Him with open hearts
We'll dwell in peace again
For no prayer goes unanswered
Unless for vulgar gain
The honest lonely heart at prayer
Will soon be free of pain

To A Friend

Whatever makes a happy time
You gave me one today
Everything we did and said
Pure joy in every way
We walked we talked
We laughed we sighed
We shared our thoughts
Abandoned pride
Our silent times were peaceful too
But all good days must end
So when it did I spoke to God
And thanked Him for a friend

Hope

Hope is the bowstring of action
Intention the pathway to goals
Dreams that are left unattended
Torture so many sad souls

Wise Men Say

Wise men talk of worlds beyond
Worlds beyond our eyes
A wondrous place of love and peace
To which the spirit flies
Wise men say we come again
To live another span
That death is just a stepping stone
A pause within the plan
Mystics say that many lives
Are needed to ensure
A perfect understanding
Of God's eternal law
Wise men say with smiling eyes
Our lives are but a dream
A brief illusion clothed in flesh
A role within a scheme
Wise men say that nothing dies
It only changes form
That life goes on despite the myth
We perish in death's storm
So when our loved ones pass away
Let hope replace our pain
Have faith and trust that God ensures
We shall all meet again

Wind Of Memory

Catch the wind of memory
Brushed gently by life's tide
Each act sealed in heartbeats
Too precious these to hide

Let them move within you
Though shame they may conceal
For these are yours forever
Your life has made them real

Our memories are treasures
Which map our earthly course
Shaping lives like flowers
Blooms of the cosmic force

For what is life but memory
Flesh does not endure
The wise soul values every step
The fool will close the door

With open heart review the pains
Exalt in pleasures spent
Each moment is a miracle
Each second only lent

I Know That You'll Be There

In face of all calamity
In trial and test through enmity
In failure and despondency
I know that You'll be there
In danger and in perplexity
In sorrow and in paucity
In fear and in aridity
I know that You'll be there
In pain and in uncertainty
In facing animosity
In grief and darkest misery
I know that You'll be there
You are the potter of my soul
You hold the secret of my goal
You validate my earthly role
I know that You'll be there
I pray to You who gave me birth
To stem the blood that stains Your earth
To raise mankind to higher worth
I know that You'll be there
My heart is sick of endless war
Which ravages the weak and poor
Let justice rout the tyrant's law
I know that You'll be there
I pray that greed and hate and spite
Shall be consumed by Your just light
And evil jailed by love's sweet might
I know that you'll be there

Just Wanted You To Know

To be content with someone
Is the greatest gift of all
To know their strengths
To know their faults
To see them rise or fall
To love them during troubled times
To share their greatest pleasures
This privilege we rarely find
When sorting through life's treasures
So I was most content with you
And wanted you to know
Despite your strengths
Despite your faults
I still do love you so.

How I Shall Miss You

How I shall miss you
Now that you've gone
The nights will be lonely
The days will be long
My love and my thoughts
Will be with you each day
My spirit beside you
In Heaven's long day
Hold close to your soul
What I have in my heart
A love that's forever
Although we're apart

Sacred Flesh

So think on this
And know it well
There is a place called hell
It dwells within the human mind
Where greed and hatred dwell
So when the cruel and testing souls
Are screaming in your ears
Just sink into your flesh and blood
And photograph their fears

I am Your Friend

For all of my life
The Whole of my life
I shall hold you in my heart
For all of my life
For the whole of my life
We'll never be apart
I cannot close my eyes
Dear heart
Yet see your lovely face
I long to be beside you
In a world of silent grace
The tide of life has washed away
The union we shared
Still death cannot deprive us
Of the memories we shared
So for all of my life
For the whole of my life
I shall hold you in my heart
And for all of my life
For the whole of my life
We shall never be apart

Mother

These flowers simply say for me
What words cannot express
God made these sweet florations
For Mother natures dress
You gave me birth and sunlight
You brought me from life's dawn
And you loved me like summer flower
From the moment I was born
Oh would it that a mothers love
Prevailed upon this earth
So words and acts of kindness
Would comfort us from birth
Then wholesome thoughts and loving deeds
Would end our mortal pain
And thoughts of greed and evil
Would never come again
For in the safety of your arms
I looked at life anew
And all the good things I possess
I owe each one to you

The Calm of Night

The calm of night is welcome now
Your love has filled my day
I am content to be alone
And dwell on what you say
Such words of joy that thrill me
That tingle through my mind
You gave me hope when hope had gone
With thoughts so warm and kind
The loneliness which I had felt
Has given way to peace
This priceless feeling came from you
And may it never cease

I've shivered through a hundred nights
Of pain and desperation
The past came whirling like a blade
Of hate and degradation
When finally my spirit died
When life no longer mattered
God sent me you with arms outstretched
To raise me bruised and shattered
You taught me how to feel again
But most importantly
You freely gave me two great gifts
Your love and company

Honours In Plenty

Do not feel sad
if you fail to succeed
Life's not a race
that is judged by its speed
Honours in plenty
so often abide
In quiet humble people
whose wealth is inside
We are urged to admire
the rich and the strong
Yet the bloodbath of history
suggests this is wrong
For those who claim more
than they rightfully need
And advocate systems
which nourish their greed
Are fearful and vain
in the lives that they live
They're able to take
but unable to give
In the souls of these people
where avarice hides

A sickness pervades
an illusion abides
This earth was not made
for the rich to gain more
It's a God given planet
we should share and adore
Life's prizes and merits
are not gifts of gold
They are spiritual gains
which can never be sold
So do not feel sad
if you fail to succeed
Life's not a race
which is judged by its speed
Honours in plenty
quite often abide
In quiet humble people
whose wealth is inside

Prickly Ride

Which are the faults which deliver our pain
Virtue brings sunshine selfishness rain
Pride heads the list on the road to distress
Followed by envy and gluttony's mess
Greed is the saddle on jealousy's back
Anger the rider intent on attack
Fear is a messenger flimsy and cruel
Turning a wise man into a fool
Meanness and arrogance hunger for wealth
Hiding the pitiful worship of self
Sloth sucks the blood of all it befriends
Lust ruins lives in pursuit of its ends
Envy ensures an insatiable ride
Through all of the faults which are headed by pride

In Peace Go Home

Through veils of peace may you ascend
To promised planes above
Where comfort shall await you
In those summerlands of love
Although my grief is deep and raw
Although my pain is great
I know that you are still with me
I know that you will wait
For in God's time we'll meet again
Of this I am quite sure
I loved you so much on this earth
In absence even more

The Deal

I realise the loneliness
That empty pain within
I share your dark vibrations
At times when faith wears thin
Yet I surely must remind you
As any friend would do
When life deals cards for the living
It deals for the dying too
We live our lives in fear of death
We shun the final hour
Clothed in black with heads hung low
We wilt before death's power
How painful are these waves of fear
These messages of doom
Which permeate the soul of man
Denying death its bloom
I beg you draw your mind around
A place beyond death's door
For all shall travel to this world
Where loved ones line the shore
They beckon us with open arms
They urge us to embrace
The wondrous world of spirit
Our home of peace and grace
For I surely must remind you
As any friend would do
When life deals cards for the living
It deals for the dying too

Many Lovely Things

In my Father's garden
Grow many lovely things
All around I see his hand
In every living thing
Look in awe
Touch with joy
Acknowledge he is king
In my Father's garden
Are many lovely things
From earth and from the ocean
From fire and from the air
He shaped his dream
A paradise supreme
For us to share
So we must love the earth
And be at one within it
To cherish every living creature
To cherish every plant and feature
In my Father's garden
Grow many lovely things
Oh so many lovely things.

Karma

Be aware you tyrants
Who cane the poor and weak
Distant eyes are watching you
And will just vengeance wreak

The pains which you so cruelly serve
On souls without defence
Shall haunt your every moment
When you have crossed life's fence

And you will cry for mercy
As cowards always do
But death shall show no mercy
Till you have suffered too

For nature calls for balance
Cruel debts are paid in pain
Each broken heart and severed limb
Will bear your guilty name

For every single human act
Has shadows in the sky
And those you killed with gun or guile
Will greet you when you die

So be aware you tyrants
You'll find no place to hide
For greater souls wait patiently
To strip away your pride

Perspective

A creator who gave us a planet as beautiful as the earth. A creator who gave us flowers sunrise, blue oceans teaming with life, magnificent forest, sweet meadows, breathtaking wildlife, soft moss, frost, breeze, rain, springtime, smells, tastes, harvests, love, inspiring passion, creativity, compassion and the smell of autumn leaves, would never be as cruel as to present us with the ever present agonies and pains of life, without a loving agenda holding a deeper meaning. It simply does not add up- it makes no sense. Earth is our college Spiritual growth our subject. Free Will our Test! Eternal Life His Promise.

Promise me

Promise me a better life
When I lay down to die
Talk to me of peaceful realms
Beyond the human lie

I wish that I could speak with joy
Of life and fruitful years
In truth I found a parody
One mostly filled with tears

When I dare view the tangled web
Which my brief life has spun
I gasp with pained indignity
At all that I have done

The many faults I carry
Have stained my spirits ride
Through mountain paths of vanity
On horses packed with pride

When hollow laughter filled my days
When youth dismissed the hours
The coat of gold I thought I owned
Decayed along with powers

I grew to rage against a God
Whose guile had sculpted life
That God who gave me happy seeds
Which blossomed into strife

Man builds - Man breaks - Man loves - Man hates
Such lessons all endure
To suffer learn and comprehend
That only death is sure

So love another where you can
Be conscious of their pain
For all are tested on the path
And most have lived in vain.

Lost Love

I wandered by the sea - the evening calm
My mind a mist of sorrow and regret
I felt the hand I love
Slip from mine
Letting go of her misfortune in an act
Cutting out her sorrows with farewell
Our memories like castles in the sand
Will wash away
Carried by the mute indifferent time or tide
Cornerstones of passion and of touch
Will live no more
Rare moments lost and blown towards the stars
That capsule which before contained all shared events
Now sags about our feet - the tension spent
What sad imperfect creatures we all are
Often serving dreams which carry us too far
Hope and heart confused and buried in debate
Watching once cherished icons decimate
Fear battled faith and faith expired
Now fear unchallenged rules without respite
Those flower strewn lanes where love and faith
Took flight.

Trust

When the doors of death are closed
The doors of heaven open
All is Well in Heaven

Nature's Wealth

A life deprived of nature
Is unnatural to us all
For nature is the body true
That mankind cannot rule
We cannot make a flower
Nor can we make a seed
We cannot make a speck of earth
From which all things proceed
The source of life is mystery
From darkness came the light
From nothingness came everything
The secret spawn of night
No human mind can penetrate
What God elects to hide
To Him the truth of origins
Forever will abide
And when He made this lovely earth
Did He feel lonely too
Placing life within the void
A gift for me and you
So beauty was our birthright
Not heartache for the self
He wanted us to know His heart
At work in nature's wealth

Oneness

I was the boy who walked on the marsh
Beneath the summer sun
I was the boy who kissed the stars
Before the earth had begun
I was the thought before the light
Which lit creations dawn
I was the love which fashioned the thought
The day the world began
I am the light the eternal light
I am the soul of man
I am the spirit which moves through the form
I am the life after death
I am the next world peaceful and calm
I am the life without breath

Worlds Entwined

He who doubts that prayer has power
Does not understand the plan
Man is linked to God through Angels
Angels are as real as man
Angels live in worlds of spirit
Realms much finer than our own
Worlds which lie beyond our seeing
Set in ether finely sown
How vain is man in blunt conclusions
All we see is what we are
All we touch is real and final
Heaven is a thought too far
What then stops the earth from falling
Not rotations idle course
How does space uphold a planet
What sustains this perfect force
Who designed the wiles of living
Who made flowers, sea and air
What great mind created matter
Made from gas in orbits rare
Objects real from our perspective
Mirror worlds we cannot see
Never doubt the world of angels
Dwelling close to you and me
For in a space of Gods designing
Where this planet has its place
Other atoms form creations
Unseen worlds of cosmic lace

To these worlds we are connected
Prayers are carried high above
Angels soothe our pains and sorrows
Turning conflict into love
Never doubt angelic forces
Help is always at your side
Pity those who mock the heavens
Sorrows are the fruit of pride

When Our Love Filled The Air

You are within me night and day
My thoughts with sadness strewn
I've lost a love that once was mine
A gift as warm as June

Once I held you bathed in fire
No passion could compare
Your soul and body beautiful
When our love filled the air

And if I ever loved before
Such memories have gone
I only hold the dream of us
It is for you I long

And in the summer of our love
Warm sunlight bathed your grace
It traced the sweetest sight I know
Your lovely lovely face

There was a garden we once shared
our love had blossomed there
Now sadness haunts this memory
Your death has left me bare

Yet I shall always love you
And when I walk alone
I shall feel you in our garden
Where those magic seeds were sown

So sweet love walk beside me
And remember how I care
For I love you now as I did then
When our love filled the air

Values

There are always shadows lurking
We will always have doubts and fears
Our dreams and aspirations
All too often end in tears
Yet life thrives upon acts of trying
It is hardship which helps us to learn
That true wealth lies in the spirit
Not in these sums we may earn.

Reviewing

When all seems lost, when life seems cruel and events unbearable, we must remember that everything is subject to change nothing is permanent! Therefore these bad times will pass and the light will shine again. Change is in the nature of things, it was ever thus. So have faith and hard as it may seem at times, look back and realise how much we have grown from past pains and testing obstacles. With all its apparent dis-ease, pain is the touchstone of spiritual growth and thus the doorway to paradise.

Love Must Rule

Much as we may seek for answers
In this world so often cruel
No one quite explains the matrix
Scholar, wise men or the fool
So in the shadows of our laughter
Lurking in each human mind
Lies the chambered fear of dying
Nature keeps her offspring blind.

If we walk towards an abyss
If nothingness is all we'll find
Loathsome is this life of struggle
Hued by something most unkind
For who would let the wicked triumph
What God would let such evil reign
Could He watch His children suffer
See them in appalling pain.
What God would let the liar prosper
Cheats and rogues live best of all
Selling sweat from honest people
Blind to every decent rule
For such it is upon this planet
Fashioned well yet left to groan
At the mercy of the villains
Ruling from their corporate throne.
Who can blame the non-believer
Snarling at a power obscure
Held by a God who feigns indifference
As the wealthy crush the poor
Yet let a heart be filled with kindness
Let mercy be anothers call
Then truth and hope and true compassion
Marks the template for us all.
For therein lies the opposition
To this path so tense and cruel
Inherent in one act of kindness
Dwells the truth that love must rule.

Natural Law

Keep it simple where you can
Selfish works are the death of man
Those who gain from devious deeds
Fill their lives with hurtful seeds
Keep it straight and keep it true
Do not judge what others do
If you swim against the tide
Into jagged rocks you'll slide
Be sure to pick a peaceful stream
To ferry you towards your dream
There's nothing wrong in aiming high
Provided you don't nurse a lie
Be careful as you go along
Not to do a person wrong
Acts of kindness kindle life
Acts of malice end in strife
Balance is the natural law
Of this one fact you can be sure
So let your scales tip to and fro
Not too high and not too low
In every single human act
Let balance be your ruling fact
Seek not ecstasy or pain
Be happy with the middle plane
And keep it simple where you can
Selfish works are the death of man

Seeing is forever

Beyond my face and form
My love
Beyond my pulse and heart
My love
Beyond my breath and blood
My love
Are things we cannot see
We've touched together
You and I
Traced out space beneath the sky
Warmed to winds that tossed the air
Kissed and mingled skin and hair
But death has called me - please don't cry
It's only the blink of an old mortal eye
It's only a sad but a loving sigh
I'll visit you at times
My love
And take your hand beside the stream
Where life persuaded us to dream
Where bluebells chimed in silent grace
And Springtime danced across your face
And now even though my existence is through
My lingering spirit will comfort you
Life is but a star
My love
That flickers for a while
It grows a little in the night
Then drops in silence from our sight
Yet in death's cherished wonderland
There writes a wise and passionate hand
Aspiring to dreams we don't understand

Memories of You

I had a drifting mood today
It stirred a thought or two
My mind went back to happy days
To memories of you
Our lives are like a tapestry
With two distinctive sides
The front a perfect picture
The back our secret hides
Our memories are built like this
Some are clear and real
Others travel in and out
With no specific feel
Life's phases too are tapestries
With textures of their own
Some we love and some we hate
From all of them we've grown
We gather wisdom from our pains
From torment we grow strong
Our spirit nurtured by mistakes
Still fated travels on
Perhaps one thing which stays the same
And will forever more
Is the love that we hold for another soul
The people we adore
So I had a drifting mood today
It stirred a thought or two
My mind went back to happy days
To memories of you

I'd Rather See You Smiling

You must not think that I have gone
Please don't grieve or pine
I'd rather see you smiling
Laughing - working - looking fine
Death is an exciting key
Which opens many doors
It leads us into other worlds
Quite similar to yours
Life is not an accident
Death is not the end
God designed a mystery
Life and death do blend
So do not think that I have gone
Please don't brood or pine
I'd rather see you smiling
Laughing - working - looking fine

To and Fro

Evening yawned as dusk was calling
Light was fading all around
Dark red paint strokes
Washed the heavens
Beams of sunlight stroked the sea

Full in soul and full of wonder
Lost in awe I turned away
In my mind's eye glimpsed the secret
Linking man to spirits of the earth

How often do we talk about where we've come from
How often do we talk about where we go
Round and round in a cloudy fishbowl
Dulled by haste we wander To and Fro

From birth to death we wander
To and Fro

Mist and darkness chase the sunlight
Evening breezes combed the fields
All this mystery still unanswered
So many paths to wander To and Fro

From birth to death we wander
To and Fro

Love And Truth

Love and truth
Are the stuff of life
They are at the moment ready
Bad memories
Will fade away
Ignore them to be steady
For life is now
Not yesterday
Tomorrow never comes
Forget what's gone or what's to come
Heed not those naked drums
Disrobe yourself of worry
Live blithe within the day
Have faith and trust
That God has planned
Your fate in every way

Song Of Life

The river flows and has no spite
Nor has the meadow flower
The breeze that dances through the corn
Is not in search of power
The birds which fill our life with song
Ask nothing in return
This loving earth can only give
And from it we should learn
We treat our planet with contempt
Like ants we do devour
The body which supports all life
For wealth for self for power
We've lost our kinship with those friends
Who roam the earth and sea
They live in fear of mortal man
Who stole their harmony
That we should look again and see
The bounties of this earth
Through eyes which see more truly
The love which gave it birth

It's So Very Sad

It's so very sad
To have lost such a friend
Since there's nothing so special
As two hearts that blend
It happens so rarely
When two people find
They share the same feeling
They're two of a kind
They may be as different
As chalk is to cheese
Yet magically sown
Is their shared sense of ease
In each others company
Life seems complete
Their joys and their sorrows
In sympathy meet
It's private and special
A privilege rare
To feel for another
To know that they care
No money can buy
What a friendship can bring
It can silver the grey skies
And make the world sing
So when counting the treasures
Which matter today
Thank God for the friendship
Which you brought my way

Lay Down Your Arms

Lay down your arms
If the pressure's too great
It's your right to change
And it's never too late
If you're always uneasy
If you've run out of hope
It's no mortal crime
To admit you can't cope
There are new doors to open
Old habits to throw
Change is the essence
If we are to grow
Your right is divine
To be here on this earth
No person is better
We are equal by birth
So acknowledge your strengths
And your weaknesses too
But don't be ashamed
Of the things you can't do

Dearest Father

Dearest Father of us all
Hear my prayer this day
Accept my life and take my will
Do with it as You may
My selfishness will hurt me
My pride will kill my joy
My greed will make me envious
For yet another toy
I cannot trust my instincts
I'm weak before their power
I cannot trust myself at all
Bad thinking rules the hour
My thoughts so often shallow
Are damaging and vain
They crowd the peace I should enjoy
Breed heartaches fear and pain
Your grace alone can soothe me
Your truth my only hope
I've learned to trust You inwardly
So doing I can cope
Since in this world so devious
I cannot turn to man
His systems are at odds with life
Fear directs his plan
This joyous garden in the air
Which You aspired to grow
Is in the hands of monsters now
Who reap but do not sow

Your garden gave me poetry
It filled me with Your song
I'll only be at peace again
When I'm where I belong
So dearest Father of us all
Hear my prayer this day
Accept my life and take my will
Do with it as You may

Why Should Death
So Final Be?

Take comfort in the ancient lore
That death is nothing but a door
Through which we enter when first sent
Through which we pass when life is spent
Our journey be it long or short
Is clothed in flesh and held in thought
And briefly do we touch sweet time
With all its pains and loves sublime
On this great planet rolled in space
Adorned by God's creative grace
Which angels fashioned long before
Mankind walked on nature's floor

There is a fashion to deny
The spirit world to which we fly
If birth and life are mystery
Why should death so final be
Perhaps the purpose of our lives
Is hidden deep by wise disguise
So may the fruits of death be great
In worlds we cannot contemplate
For what the human eye can't see
Should not be judged a fallacy
So little do we comprehend
How life and death may sweetly blend

Child Of The Planet

Avoid all loud and greedy people
Let them travel on
You'll find the air about you sweeter
Once the proud have gone
And in this changing turgid world
Be faithful to your heart
And stand against adversity
Though hopes may fall apart
And stand aside from those who sneer
Who label life a trick
So many minds are poisoned
So many minds are sick
You'll find this world is full of strife
But try and understand
That side by side with misery
There sits a loving hand
So call on God when times are bad
And thank Him when they're fine
In gratitude lies plenitude
Let faith become your wine

It Will Pass

I know how you feel
In the dark lonely hours
When the comfort of day never comes
I know what it's like to be blown in a wind
Of misgivings and sorrowful pains
Tossed like a leaf your mind is adrift
With confusion and utter despair
You ache with a pain that nothing can soothe
You cry out and there's nobody there
Yes I know how it feels
To be endlessly sad
Alone in a dungeon of gloom
Nothing is real but the fear that's inside
And the dread of tomorrow's grey bloom
You've been robbed of the one
Who brought joy to your life
You feel angry deserted and lost
But your sorrow will lessen
Your grieving will end
And perhaps you will cherish this truth
In the fulness of time
We shall all meet again
In a world without hardship and pain
So talk to your love
Who has passed through the veil
Don't dismiss them because they're away
Remember to tell them to brush-up the mat
You'll be wiping your feet on one day

Keep It Simple

Thank-you Father for this day
The lovely things you brought my way
My home my friends my family
The gift to hear the eyes to see
A garden where sweet flowers grow
A place to love in sun or snow
I was a slave to complex life
Which brought my spirit endless strife
Now I thank you for simplicity
I thank you for allowing me

To live my life in harmony
Devoid of sham and drudgery
To know that I can always turn
To you at times when I must learn
To keep life simple come what may
And live my life within the day
No yesterdays must cloud my joy
No future fears my heart employ
I take each day as you decree
I'm truly rich for knowing thee

Just As The Sun

Just as the sun
Must surely rise
Just as the moon shall wane
Just as the night shall follow day
Just shall we suffer pain
Just as life's scales
Should balance true
So must our lives accord
Tipped to extremes by selfish dreams
Greed negates reward
Just as life
Is ours to live
So death is God's to claim
Let fairness rule your every thought
Let justice be your aim
Just as pride breeds lives unreal
So greed erodes the soul
No one owns one single speck
Of God Almighty's whole
Just as love transcendeth all
So envy will devour
Man's rights to freedom on this earth
As evil spreads its power
Just as life
Is ours to live
So death is God's to claim
Be kind to others and yourself
Let justice be your aim

Follow Your Dreams

Follow your dreams
Whatever they are
Let no one turn your head
It's a very short time you're living
Too short to be hampered by dread
Don't listen to those who will tell you
That your dreams are impractically spun
You can't live the life of another
You'll never get anything done
So cherish your goals and ambitions
They're given to you to fulfil
A voice deep within can be trusted
To guide you and strengthen your will
There's nothing that you cannot conquer
There's nothing you cannot achieve
If your heart has a need
And your mind finds the seed
Harness hope and you're bound to succeed

Dawn

Slowly saw the sun ascending
Through a veil of pink and grey
Watched the sea mist stalk the cliffside
Saw it swirl and puff and play
Walking on through shaded coppice
Heard the mellow sounds of life
Breathing in a dampened hedgerow
Soaring in the swallows' flight
Felt the speed of running water
Touched the loneliness of light
Held a moist leaf cool and peaceful
Cool and peaceful from the night
Out again and into sunlight
Passed the yellow hissing corn
Passed the singing waving barley
On to pond and reed and spawn
High above the lark is sounding
High above she views the earth
Higher still the clouds are shading
Lark and spawn and silent birth

First Things First

Easy does it
Slowly feel your way
Don't rush a single thing
Always pray
First things first
Live within the day
Never mind tomorrow
You only live today
The past had gone forever
The future's never here
Surrender to this simple truth
You'll never live in fear
Fear is caused by things we've done
Or things we hope to do
Fear is thought in chaos
Fear distorts our view
So live just in the one day
Forget those future woes
The past is past is past now
And tomorrow never shows
This day is eternity
It's shaped and mapped for you
Live it by the grace of God
That's all you're asked to do

When compassion and caring are directed at a soul in distress, then the highest attributes of humanity are expressed.

Although, at times it is difficult to believe, I think the purpose of our earthly life is to grow in spiritual awareness. Paradoxically, pain is often our tutor.

I know that in life we must all face death but it is also my passionate belief that in death we shall discover life abundant.

Do No Harm
Surely this is the law and the whole law.